D1474995

Critical Thinking and Self-Awareness: How to Use Critical Thinking Skills to Find Your Passion: Plus 20 Questions You Must Ask Yourself

Steven West

Published by Steven West, 2019.

CRITICAL THINKING AND SELF-AWARENESS: HOW TO USE CRITICAL THINKING SKILLS TO FIND YOUR PASSION: PLUS 20 QUESTIONS YOU MUST ASK YOURSELF

First edition. July 17, 2019.

Copyright © 2019 Steven West.

ISBN: 978-1393179634

Written by Steven West.

Critical Thinking and Self-Awareness:
How to Use Critical Thinking Skills to Find Your Passion
Plus 20 Questions to Find Your Strengths

Chapter One: Learning What Critical Thinking Is

Critical thinking is a big part of one's decisions and intellectual thought process, but many people don't know how to train themselves to do it or utilize the benefits that come with it once they can. It is a very important and helpful tool for helping us find out who we are and what we would like out of life. It can be complicated to learn for some people and harder for others but it's a very good tool to have in your mental arsenal as it can make your thought processes better than it already is. Many people find that they are not happy with their current jobs or pursuits. Oftentimes, they question their place in the world, even going so far as having an identity crisis or the dreaded midlife crisis. These days, millennials are having what they call 'quarter-life crisis' where they are questioning their place in this world at a much younger age.

In today's society, the number of people trying to find their passions, what they want out of life, and trying to find their place seems to have skyrocketed. The key critical thinking skills can be used to help us figure out how to help ourselves find what it is that we really want from our lives and it can also help us understand what it is that we're seeking in our lives. This will also answer the question of where we belong and where our place in the world is. Because our passions can help us discover what it is that we really love to do, and what we want to spend our time doing, critical thinking is a vital tool to help us determine these things. Once we've learned how to utilize critical thinking skills and where our passions lie, we can begin to follow our passions in our daily lives, whether it be a career or a hobby or just anything that we feel a real passion for deep down.

But first things first, the definition of critical thinking itself helps us better understand exactly what thought process and skills we would be utilizing, and it is hard to understand just what we're talking about if we don't know what the definition is. The definition of critical thinking lets us know that critical thinking is making logical and well thought out judgments and making reasoned judgments. This simply means, instead of making rash decisions, you are thinking about the information you have received and not just accepting the information that's given to you. It also means you're questioning other conclusions. Critical thinking is said to be the most successful form of thinking when it comes to effectively combining our feelings and senses with our logic and intuition. This would prove vital in helping us realize our passions and skills in life.

It is also said that critical thinking can help students learn better. It has become the most effective tool for college students to find better careers or help adults already in the job force find better careers if they are not happy in their current one or find more success and happiness in the job that they're already in. This is because this skill set helps us become more insightful and trust our instincts. Trusting yourself is always something that can be improved on and it's a big part of the critical thinking process.

A perfect example of this thought process would be a child that still believes in Santa Claus. He/she would believe that it was Santa that put their presents under the Christmas tree and not their parents who put the presents under the tree, based upon the stories that their parents had told them from childhood. Because they've heard of this since they were a child, they trust and accept the information given to them and don't question any other possible outcome. However, a critical thinker would be able to determine that Santa Claus does not, in fact, exist and that the logical conclusion would be that their parents had indeed put the packages under the Christmas tree themselves. Critical thinking helps you separate fact from fiction and the truth from lies. Simply accepting the facts presented to you and never questioning, you never realize anything new, or anything different. You never form your own thoughts or identity because you're simply going along with everything everyone tells you, accepting lies as truth, or whatever anyone says as truth. Critical thinking helps us to learn how to become smarter about what we know and what we learn. That's one of the reasons why learning how to become a critical thinker is complicated for some people.

Another example could be the 'Tooth Fairy'. Many parents tell their children that this creature exists when it doesn't. But no one stops to think that this is not real because their parents have told them it was. A non-questioning person or child obviously wouldn't question it. Why would they? They accept what their parents say and keep believing all they want. But remember, we are using critical thinking to help find our passions and strengths. One of the biggest things we need to remember is that we question the information being presented to us and think of logical conclusions. Do we really have nothing to say about a magic fairy who flies every night into bedrooms taking young people's teeth? No, probably not. We would question what they're telling us and be able to conclude that the Tooth Fairy does not exist and once again, it's our parents doing the sneaking in with our teeth. We would begin to think about this logically. What makes more sense? A flying fairy taking people's teeth, or that your parents are giving you money for losing your teeth. That is how we would be able to conclude the truth. Obviously, there are many scenarios in which we should question and seek out every possible conclusion. These are a couple that is easy to understand and picture while still understanding the basic concept of critical thinking.

By teaching yourself to become a better critical thinker, it will be easier to utilize your skills for a better professional career and help you if you're in school as well. Someone who utilizes their thinking skills can approach problems in a more systematic and consistent way while understanding the link between ideas. This is very useful if you're in college because the way you think will help you get a better career once your schooling days are over. If you're already working, this can help you have better ideas and stronger opinions to present. They can also appraise and recognize arguments while understanding the importance and relevance of these ideas and arguments. You will also be able to determine the relevance and importance of arguments in your daily life. After being able to determine these things, you will be able to reflect on your justification of your beliefs, values, and assumptions.

Now that we've discussed the benefits of critical thinking and now that we know what it actually is, we can begin to discuss the skills needed to start the process of becoming a better thinker. The first thing that helps us in this process is to begin thinking of a topic, any topic you're dealing with, or just any topic in general, in a critical and objective way.

Step two would be to identify the differentiating arguments that you're facing or that others are facing in relation to this particular issue and argument. After the identification, you should evaluate your point of view and realize how strong or valid your feelings and point may be. Are there any negative points or weaknesses in the evidence of your point? Be aware that there might be. We also need to be aware that there could be implications behind what we're saying in our statement. After going through this process, we should also provide reasoning that has been structured and support the point that we're trying to make.

These skills will help you become a better critical thinker. However, an important thing to realize is that while these tips will help you become a more critical thinker, no one thinks critically all the time. It can depend on many factors. While critical thinking has been said to be the perfect combination of thoughts and feelings helping you to control both, too much emotion can lead to rash decisions and impulsivity which can cause a negative effect. Using critical thinking is a way to balance these things and not let one rule the other. By being rash and impulsive, we tend to quickly let our emotions rule and we're not thinking of our actions. This can cause us to make decisions we might regret later. Emotions are a wonderful thing and I am not saying emotional decisions are bad. I am merely saying that using your thinking skills and your emotions are a better way to go. The good news in these situations is that once we've started to begin the process of trying to apply critical thinking in our lives, we can develop better routines and activities and begin to apply these skills to problems we face daily which helps us make better decisions.

Another good example of using the skills we just mentioned would be a business owner. Let's say a business owner decides to move his business to a new location. This sounds like a wonderful idea and one assumes that this would be an amazing opportunity with untapped potential. However, when you begin to use the thought process we outlined, questions begin to arise. Do not accept the information you've been given without thought. Remember, we are thinking logically about every possible conclusion and if we just rush into it based on emotion, then we're not following the steps as we should, and this could be opening the door for conflicts and negativity. This would be a very big decision for the business owner to make. So, he really needs to take the time to think it through. It would affect his livelihood and the people that work for him. It could affect his customers and even his family if things go wrong. Then, the business owner begins to ask questions. Is the travel distance to the new location very far? What if the people that work for him can't make the distance or it puts a strain on them? Will you lose customers in this location? Is this the best idea for his budget? Rash decisions and not thinking it through would simply take the opportunity by not stopping to think about whether this is the best idea.

For the sake of this example, to show a possible negative effect from his choice, we will say that the owner rushed the decision without thinking critically. He goes ahead with the deal and runs into complications. The new location is too far for his workers to get there and one by one he losses them and he has to hire more. Then he runs into more complications and after a point, he has to close down the new location and is now back at square one. Or he might not have a store any longer, at all. A critical thinker, however, is weighing the options and trying to see if there is a way to lessen potential conflict or negative impact in the situation while understanding the weaknesses and strengths that lie in their argument. Applying critical thinking steps help this business owner make a much more informed decision and because he's making a more informed decision, he is much less likely to get into trouble or have a negative impact because of his decisions. In scenario two, if he still had to close his business or lose the location, the decision was much more informed, and he had all the facts before deciding. However, because he was more informed, he was much less likely to fall into a negative complication and therefore, would be less likely to fall into losing his business.

Sometimes it may be difficult to do this because a lot of times critical thinking forces a person to take an internal look at yourself. It will help you access your weaknesses and strengths, your possible impact with your decisions, and help you understand your preferences. It also forces you to review possible results of your decisions and possible changes you need to make to the decisions that you've made in your life. This can be very hard because taking that deep of a look inside ourselves can be difficult and make us see things or face things we may not want to. When changing your decisions, you can avoid negative outcomes and then the impact will be lessened. These thinking skills and step by step process for thinking things through helps us make better choices in a more positive manner and lessen the chances of a negative impact on our lives.

Another reason critical thinking is hard is that, for a lot of people, their world is black and white. When you begin to think critically, that black and white fade away and the lines become less simple as you become more self-aware and sincerer in your beliefs and thoughts. Remember that using your critical thinking steps also helps you become a more insightful thinker and it's going to help you become a stronger thinker. This is a useful skill that is going to help you in school and in life. They say that one of the things they love in the job force now is someone who has mastered their mind and has good critical thinking skills because it's the type of problem-solving thinking that truly can help you in the workforce today.

Chapter Two: Learning to Use Critical Thinking in Everyday Life

Critical thinking can not only help us find our true passions in life, but it can also help us learn how to own our lives and become more self-aware. Media these days plays a big part in our thinking as so do our friends. But we need to be aware that they do not know everything. We should be able to discern what's true and what's not. These days, most people can't tell the difference between what they see on their feed on social media websites or a legitimate story. Videos on these sites can be misleading as well. Our social media sites have so much information flowing on them that people see thousands of posts a day or videos full of information. What's real and what's not? How do we tell the truth?

I have had friends scroll through their feed and find something they thought was real and post it only to have all of their friends leave horrible comments and tell her it wasn't real. She was embarrassed and hurt. If she had waited and thought the situation through, instead of just accepting what she read or what she was told, it could have been avoided. The stories sounded ligament too. See, this is why it's so important to hone those critical thinking skills so we don't get taken in by false information and so we can help others from falling for things like that as well.

Likewise, most people listen to their friends and think a certain way or act a certain way because it's accepted as cool or we're told we're supposed to think that way. Cliques and groups of friends can be detrimental in this way because you're not thinking about how you'd like to think, you're thinking how they tell you to think. That's not helping you in putting your skills to use. One friend might tell you it's cool to smoke, another might hate a political person and tells you that have to as well to be friends with them.

In the high school and college world, even in the younger world these days, there are so many cases where people have friends that tell them that they have to do something and when we don't question and just go along with it, we lose ourselves and who we really are. They are trying to make you think what they think even though you're a unique individual with your own thoughts and ideas. If you're conforming to other's way of thinking instead of your own, you're not being yourself.

When we are younger, in most cases with friends or even family, we would not want to question the information we are given because we could be too afraid of the consequences of acting that way or speaking our mind. In this case, it's because your friends think one way and are telling you that you have to think that way too, you do not want to question anything for fear of losing a friend. What you need to realize, however, is that some friends can have negative effects on us and if they're trying to force you into thinking a way you don't want to, or never let you have opinions of your own, it's probably not a good friendship in the first place. Critical thinking allows us to see the negative impact and consequences of our decisions. In using this skill, you would probably arrive at the conclusion that this is not a very good friendship to have and it may be doing more harm than good in your life.

In the adult world, you might be at a job where everyone is thin, and they tell you that you need to lose weight or something of that nature. If everyone in the office thinks a certain way about issues they've seen on the news or the internet and you don't, would you feel obligated to say you did? You might because you wouldn't want to be ostracized. With your skills though, would you really agree? Or, would you, after thinking it logically and questioning it, have a different opinion? With peer pressure in the teenage world and the adult world, people need to be able to think for themselves and not fall into the trap of thinking what every else does. We need to be able to think and see the world around you on your own terms. This is especially true for younger people. They get told so many things and have so much information and most never question the world around them. Believing in Santa Claus or the Tooth Fairy until their teenage years, that's an innocent example; however, most of the information our youth receives is not, and critical thinking would benefit them as well because they would learn to question the world around them and be curious.

The younger generation is exposed to the media, not just in the televised form, but also on smartphones, social media apps, and websites. It's telling them information every minute and youth can have a very hard time separating the fact from the fiction. Even some adults face that sometimes. Critical thinking could play a very big part in helping this problem because it teaches us to question and come up with the best conclusion and reduce negativity from our choices. By looking at every conclusion, you can vastly narrow down issues that might arise from the choices you're making. They would have been able to practice critical thinking for years if they're taught how to do it at a young age. By the time they made it into the adult world, they would have probably mastered their own minds, which is a skill I am sure we'd all like to have as it can be massively helpful in both the academic and professional world.

Even if you're not ready to say your opinions on your own terms when you're with your friends, co-workers, or family, you can still change your thinking. Every situation literally has dozens of different outcomes but critical thinking can help you redefine them and think them through much better than if you weren't using critical thinking at all.

Many people have different opinions on what they think or believe in this world and if you honestly feel like you can't speak your mind, you're probably not in the friendships you need in your life and need to make some important decisions. An important aspect of critical thinking is realizing the consequences and implications of an action of yours or beliefs. At its core, critical thinking in everyday life can help you to form your own set of beliefs on everything, from what you think about your religion to what you think about your career. Critical thinking is an important tool to use in our lives because it makes us more self-aware and can help us become more insightful while helping us discover who we are and what we believe. In short, this style of thinking can be complicated because it can make you rethink about just about everything and you could find your belief system totally changed. This isn't a bad thing, but it definitely takes some getting used to. A bonus is that when this changes your beliefs and thoughts, you're firmer in them because you've taken the time to really talk to yourself, know yourself, and thought things through. So, it's not on a whim that you're thinking this. It's because you've taken the time to realize how you really feel about it.

A good time to practice your thinking skills is to use the time you have during the day where you're not busy. We all have time in the day where we do nothing or use our time less productively than we could. During a time when we're watching television or taking a bath, you could be going through the steps of critical thinking to hone your skills. We sit in traffic on the way to work, in most cases, some people sit there for at least an hour; or wait at the doctor's office which we all know that in here, the waiting could take two or three hours; we go to activities where we have to wait for people; or even while you're cooking dinner and let your mind wander; there's a lot of opportunities to become a better thinker. So, by trying to use the time in this way, you're using your time more productively and you'll feel less like you're wasting time. We can analyze situations and see where we went wrong and what could have been done differently.

They say after an argument or discussion, you always think 'I should have said this', or 'I should have handled it this way'. We all have moments like this. In every situation, we all have moments where we regret things that we've done and wish that we had done things differently. With critical thinking being put into place, we can realize what decisions should have been made in those situations and how we could have handled them better. This will help us begin to use our skills better and, in the future, you may be able to use your thinking skills to have the situation play to how you want it. It will also help you feel better because a lot of people have regrets over arguments like that and if you start thinking things through, you can cut down on feeling bad about what you should have done and learn how to do it the way you want instead.

Keeping a journal is another way to help you become a better thinker. Skeptical? Hear me out. A journal is not just a way to release stressful feelings or write the innermost secrets you can't tell anyone else. It can be used as a device to help you learn and fix mistakes or decisions you've made. When you think 'I should have handled it better', write down why. How would you have handled it if you were thinking critically? When you write these down more and more while you're in the process of becoming a better thinker, you'll become more familiar with your patterns and how you handle situations. Using your journal and recording this situation, you will notice that in your daily life, you will start to handle the situations better than before and you'll use your critical thinking more often. You've been studying your journal entries daily and thinking daily that the process will become easier as you keep doing it. Day by day, you'll see that you're able to see how you want to handle an argument and find it easier to handle it the way that you choose to instead of how you did before.

Another thing we can practice with critical thinking is to separate fact from fiction. Remember, above I said that most people these days can't tell a fake story on social media from a true story on the news. When listening to a friend or college as they tell you a story, you don't need to accept everything as factual. Hesitate and think for a moment about how much does your friend know about what they're talking about? How much do you?

Let's use a simple example. Your friend says that she read a story on social media that says Big Foot is real and that he was spotted in the mountains living in a cave. She immediately comes to tell you because she thinks it's a really cool story. So, instead of researching, she comes to tell you because she's so excited. Is she an expert on Big Foot? How much does she really know about him? In the sentence above, we said she didn't research at all to see if the story was true. So, she's not critically thinking at all and is just accepting everything as truth. What about you? How much do you know about Big Foot? Did they get the information from a reputable source? Most people assume certain magazines are better than others and that some are truthful while others are gossip rags. Are you able to determine rightfully which ones are and which ones aren't? Websites can be favorited as well, and some people will swear until they are blue in the face that everything they read from a certain place is the absolute final truth and they can't be swayed to think anything else. Some people are set in their convictions and that's fine. But you need to use your critical thinking skills to determine what's real and what's not.

Is it really? The source they swear by. Is it really as legitimate as they said? Think about it. Does it really seem like a credible source? Or does it seem a little too farfetched? The example I used had specific details. Big Foot was spotted in a cave in the mountains. Already I have questions just thinking about this scenario. Which mountains? What cave? Why is he living in a cave? See, you still have questions. Just because someone swears it's true doesn't mean it is and this is where our skills come into play. Look at everything logically and follow our steps to reach the truth. You don't have to be rude and tell them you think they're wrong, but you don't have to believe it all either and can form your own opinion about the conversation. You can tell them politely that your opinion is different without upsetting anyone or causing conflict and exchange your ideas and talk about what they mean. Are these facts real that your friend is presenting to you or is it just other people's opinions?

The same can be said if you have to work in a group of people. Let's say you work at an office. Your group is in charge of coming up with a plan for a new update for your software. A colleague of yours is excited because he has a great idea for an update and he swears it's going to revolutionize your company. He's so sure of his plan and so excited that it's hard to not get swept up in his enthusiasm. But remember, we have to think this through. Has he thought it through? Does it seem too good to be true? Maybe his plan seems too hasty? Maybe this isn't the best course of action for your group. Does anyone else have any ideas for your group? Present your concerns in a polite manner and raise your own ideas. You could do an investigation on your own and raise your own questions as well. While you're doing that, you can see your own facts and solutions. Do they work better for your group? Are they more thought out than the other solutions your group has offered? We're not discrediting your colleague. Were simply saying maybe his way isn't the best way for your group. We're not being rude to him or anything like that, we're simply wondering if this has been thought through. When we are critically thinking, it makes us question things and that's a good thing, but we have to remember that not everyone is utilizing the same thought process you are.

Or maybe, your first colleague's idea was for the best and now you all feel better because you've thought it out. Instead of just settling for a quick fix solution, you've thought it out logically and studied all the options that were presented to you. This could lead to organizational success and career success as well. Challenging the status quo might help you become better at what you do, and it will help you utilize your thinking skills as you're still practicing becoming a better critical thinker. Trust yourself and your instincts and abilities to access situations, make informed and intelligent conclusions and analyze data. Be sure to be polite and kind when you're presenting your ideas as you don't want anyone to be rude or upset with you. This doesn't mean you have to back down from your ideas. Just be kind and if your opinion differs from other people, tell them. You might be able to help someone else use critical thinking skills and help them become more insightful and self-aware in their own life.

This is a good personal experiment to use in your daily life. You're testing new ideas and thinking skills that will help you in all aspects of your life and daily routines. From your career to your interests, you can begin to make better decisions and even find hidden passions that you had no idea you were even interested in.

Insightful thinking is also a bonus from practicing thinking. Becoming an insightful thinker is a good mental tool for you as well. Insightful thinking is also useful because it allows you to think deeper and be more perceptive not just in your thoughts but the world around you. Compare it to learning to dance the salsa. If you're not used to the dance, you wouldn't be amazing right away. Right? But with practice and diligence, you'd get better over time. Likewise, with critical thinking, the more you practice it, the better you get. The better you get, the easier it is to use it in your daily life and master your mind. It may seem like a lot to go through and you might be wondering if this is all worth it, but it is. The skills that you develop from beginning to use thinking skills like this can benefit your whole life.

Every choice we make could turn to critical thinking. Think about your health. You want to have a new exercise program or a new diet so that you can be a healthier person, or to live longer, but which will you choose? There're dozens of diets every day. Not all of them are safe. Some can be dangerous and have been proven to cause damage to people's bodies or make people end up hospitalized, but some of them are safe. Some diets or exercises are recommended and have been proven to be useful and very helpful to people while improving their lives which is what you want in the first place to make your life better.

Just like some diets are better for certain people, there are exercises that are better for some people than others as well. You have to decide what's best for you. A woman with a hysterectomy, for example, would be a good example. Her core wouldn't be as strong because she just had surgery. If she had had the surgery recently, which we will say she has for the sake of this example, then lifting weights wouldn't be a good idea right away. Not to mention she could severely hurt herself and cause further damage and end up in a hospital. But if someone told her it was, she might be tempted to try it because that was what she was told. If she didn't question the information given to her, she could severely hurt herself and ruin her recovery. If she used critical thinking skills and questioned the information she was given, her opinion would be different. If she questioned doctors or experts, they would tell her that she has to wait for a good amount of time after such an operation before even attempting such a feat and that she can't lift at all for at least three months or longer and even then, only small amounts. She would be smart and ignore that person's advice after hearing the advice of the professionals and experts in the field.

Apply your thinking skills here in both situations. Remember, logical thinking, pros, and cons, think of these carefully. Go over the information you've been presented and think about where the information comes from. Is it reputable? Does it seem too good to be true? Many companies these days swear they have the answer. Is it the answer for you or is it not what you need? You need to come to your own conclusions. This world has so much information every second every day that it can become so overwhelming to even think about. Once again, however, by utilizing these skills, you can narrow the information down and keep from getting overwhelmed or getting stressed.

Looking into a career, critical thinking comes into play here too. Using your thinking skills that helped in leading you into your passion, you can choose a career you really care about. You need to be able to assess what the best situation is for what you want to do. I am going to use the writer example again. You're very passionate about writing and it's what you know you want to do for the rest of your life. You're presented with a vast amount of information right away. There are jobs that are real while others are a scam. Others still are such good scams that sometimes we don't even realize it is. It's up to you to use your skills to weed through all the information and find the truth of what you're searching. Is your passion leading you to freelance? Writing a novel? Being a blogger? For some people, being in the limelight makes them happy. They could choose journalism or a career that's more up front. Learn the truth of what you want to do and where to best utilize your skills while letting you follow your passion and make you happy. Find reputable places to work and make sure that you're making the best decision for yourself while following your passion and staying true to yourself.

With critical thinking, it becomes a little easier to do this. You know yourself better, your beliefs, and values. You begin to see things in a different light. While researching, seek out experts. Keep in mind, experts are not always experts. You have to do the research to make sure the expert is an actual expert. Someone could say that they are and then you research it and find out that they're just a blogger or someone behind a computer screen pretending to be someone official. There are even places these days where you can buy certificates that say anything you want them to. So, it's very important to pay attention and listen and question what we're told. Use your skills to understand what you're being told and figure out what the truth is. When doing the research, you have to be sure that they are, in fact, who they say they are. When we go to the doctor, we assume that because they have a Ph.D. that they are an expert in their field and can answer our questions and give us a proper analysis. If we heard over fifty doctors or professors say the same thing and all agree about what they're saying, you would think that there was something to what they're talking about and you would probably believe what they said after conducting your own research on the topic. You'd be able to come up with your own analysis and form your own opinions about the information you have been told.

It helps you realize that people can manipulate you. The world around you can as well. Unfortunately, the world around us had a lot of people that only care about themselves and they take pride in lying and deceit. You need to understand this because if you don't, you could get hurt. It can feed you information that can be completely false and tell you it's true and have you stress and worry about things that aren't even real. Social media doesn't help because it feeds us more information more than anything else. Pages are updated every day. New stories come out every day. Everyone has an opinion, and some claim their opinions are facts when they're nothing more than one-person thoughts.

Learning to separate fact and fiction can be a tricky process and take time but the benefits of taking the time are worth it. You won't get fooled into believing things that aren't real and can come up with your own mind. This helps you become a stronger person. When we begin to question and use our thinking skills, the black and white will fade and lines will blur, but you will see things for yourself. As children, we don't really question much of anything. We do the basics that all children do. Why is the sky blue, why do I have to sleep, but we don't ask important questions like why do people lie on social media? How do I protect myself? Things like that. Now, these small questions can lead to bigger things later but usually, it takes a while for us to get to that point. This is another reason I believe that starting with critical thinking while you're younger can majorly benefit your life.

Logic will prevail. You will be able to determine what is real and what isn't with what you see and hear, and with what you're told and what you think. Using these skills can benefit you so much and these are definitely worth practicing in your life to make you more insightful and aware of the world around you. Remember, it may seem complicated at first, but if you keep practicing your thinking skills, it gets easier over time. I cannot stress enough how useful this skill is to have in your mental arsenal. It's so beneficial for your life and it can benefit your friends and family if they want you to help. You could teach them the benefits and let them experience how to train their minds too. In this way, their black and white world can fade away too as they begin to see what critical thinking helps you achieve.

Chapter Three: Learning to Differentiate Between Strength and Passion and How Strength Can Lead to Passion

Many people who want to find their passion stop to think, what am I good at? What are my skills? Therein lies the question of, what are my strengths? I believe that knowing your strengths can lead you to your passion and that the two can go hand in hand to creating happiness in your life. As before, with critical thinking, the best way to understand strength and passion is to first define what they are and the differences between the two, so we can better understand what it is we're describing. Many people can get the two confused and they are actually quite different when you know what they mean.

The definition of strength simply tells us that strength is the act of being strong. For our needs, this is not a very helpful definition. However, if you read further, it says a legal, logical, or moral force. Personal strength, however, might be closer to what we're looking for. Personal strength refers more to the skills you possess. It is said that strengths are actions or tasks that you do well. This can include knowledge or skills, or even the talents you possess. Because of the definition of personal strength, we're now able to use the first definition we came across. Think of your strengths as a strong personal skill.

An example of a strength could be playing the flute or being a really good public speaker. These are things that you do well and are good at. So, by the definition we just read, this lets you know that these things are strengths that you possess because you're good at them. People can use these skills and traits in their daily lives to relate easily to other people, or complete goals and work that they have. Because strength can have so many different meanings, it can be tricky to understand what you're dealing with. For what we're dealing with, to help us find our passion, it's this definition of personal strength that is going to be the most useful and beneficial to us. It will also be the definition that is easiest for us to understand. Passion is a strong feeling of enthusiasm or excitement, either to do something or for something. It's also an ambition that has materialized into actions. Passion for life is anything that motivates, challenges, or intrigues you. The definitions of strength and passion are pretty different, right? Yes and no. Remember what I had said earlier. I believe that knowing your strengths will help you find your passions. So, let's look at it like this. Do you remember Billy? He had the strength for learning and as he learned, he loved history. Now, he also had a passion for it but right now, we're just going to look at the strength. He was already good at learning. Because he was, he used that skill and found his passion for history and then turned it into a great career. Other people are lucky enough to find their passion right away and don't have to wait at all to find it like the example of Suzy and the violin.

Now, if we remember her story, she had the passion to play the violin, but she didn't have the strength of skill to play it like she wanted to. But it was her eventual strength. After practicing and learning how to make herself better, she became really good and her passion was taken even further because she was able to play better. This is another good case of passion and strength going hand and hand. If Suzy had given up on the violin which was her passion and what she loved to do, she would have been unhappy and less fulfilled because she wouldn't be doing what she loved. So, instead, she decided to work hard and turn a strength that wasn't very strong and made it a good skill. Now she's happy and fulfilled in her life and she's able to follow her passions.

Another thing that we can think about is that a strength can also be a passion and vice versa. Let's use the flute thing again. If you play the flute well and you love to do it and it makes you happy, then it's both a strength and a passion. Remember that a strength is something you're good at and passion is something that excites you. In this case, it's both. This can help a lot when you're trying to figure out what your strengths and passions are. Oftentimes, if they coincide, it makes it easier to figure things out and it works really well because, in most cases, it's something you're already doing so it's easier to find. In others, however, you have to find the strengths and passions and that's okay as well. The path to finding your strengths and passions can be really fun and it's a really cool way to learn self-discovery.

The skills we learn in our life are not just to find jobs or careers. That is what we all use them for and it's a good thing to do, of course, but that is not the only thing that your skills are good for. If we recognize our skills early on, any time you recognize them would be fine but if you do it earlier, you'd obviously get to utilize them longer and be able to benefit from them longer, then we can begin to use them to help us find our passion in life. This is also where critical thinking comes back into play. Remember that when we begin to use critical thinking, we're systematically thinking things through both logically and thinking of all of the possible conclusions. We're also trying to lessen the chance of negative impact and make our decisions to the best of our ability instead of rash decisions and not thinking things through.

A good thing to remember is that critical thinking can take some getting used to. A lot of times, based on emotions or circumstances, we jump to quick decisions, and we don't think our decisions through. Often, this leads to negative consequences. Remember the business owner. We had described how he had thought things through but we focused on the possible outcomes if he hadn't remembered what happened. His business shut down or he'd have to go back to the original location because he hadn't thought things through. Or he'd lose his store completely because he jumped too quickly on his decision before thinking about the ramifications of his decisions. This is not to say impulsive decisions are one hundred percent bad. Some work very well. But unfortunately, most don't because you're running strictly on emotion, and not necessarily with enough logic. Remember, critical thinking is the best combination of the two. It helps us make the best logical decisions possible. It's been said that critical thinking helps us master our mind and helps understand emotions. This way, when we begin to use this in our life, we understand how to control our emotions better and make better decisions that benefit us instead of making quick decisions that ultimately end up causing more harm than good.

The difference between strengths and passions would be that strengths are the tools that we need to use, and passion is the fuel that we need to keep ourselves going. We can have all the passion in the world, but we still need the tools to make the fuel work. Remember that the difference between passion and strength is that passion is the motivation and the drive for something you're excited and care about, and strengths are the skills we have at our disposal. Think of it like a car. Passion would be the gas while our strengths would be the car. The car wouldn't work without gas, and if the gas didn't have the car, it would have nothing to fill up. Our strengths and passions together make us stronger because when you have both, they work well together helping you create a career you'll love. They can also help you find hobbies or loves in our lives that we wouldn't have thought about in other senses and it can open a whole new world to us full of new possibilities and amazing things that can help us feel more fulfilled.

Using our passions for hobbies can help us learn new things that can help us in our daily lives and routines as well. Learning new hobbies can also help us in the professional field as well in ways that are both surprising and unexpected. For instance, if you find you have a passion for languages, that could vastly improve your resume and career path because being bilingual or trilingual is an amazing thing and everyone is needing people with those skills. Or, if you had a passion for helping people, there are thousands of ways you could do this to fulfill your passions, or if you were wishing a career choice that helps people, your options are endless there too. Everything from nursing to teachers, there are all sorts of careers where you can help people and follow the passions of your heart.

This is a good example of why figuring out your strengths and passions can be so important. It may not seem like an important thing to think about but when you do, you begin to realize just what it is. We all have passions and strengths, but we don't always utilize them, and in a lot of cases, many people find that when they understand what their passions and strengths are, they are more fulfilled and happier in their lives because they've found something they really love and haven't given up on it. Or, they feel fulfilled because they may have felt something was missing in their lives and then they found their passion. When a person finds their passion and they get to experience it, they may have felt their soul tell them that this thing, whatever it is that they found, is right, that it feels right, and they could have found what they've been missing. This can make their lives a lot better and cut down on stress or feeling lost if they find the passions that they've been looking for, and once they're able to begin following them, they can find that they also feel their time is being much better spent.

Everyone in life wants to know where they belong and what it is that they like to do or what makes them happy. This leads them on a search for what their passion is in life. Some people have one passion some have many. It's all about finding out for yourself. Everyone is different and what works for someone else might not work for you because we all have a different makeup, different thoughts, ideas, and personalities. So, when you're looking for your passion, you may share a love of something with a friend, but just because they like it doesn't mean you have to as well. It doesn't mean you can't, but it just means that you shouldn't force yourself to like something just because everyone else around you do. If you do that, you're compromising yourself and no one should do that to themselves.

In either case, our passions can lead to strength and our strengths can lead to passion. But it helps to know the difference between the two to utilize them to their best advantage. Some strengths were learned at a young age while others were learned later as we grow and develop, but they can still be used to help you discover what and where your passions are, and where they lie. Some of the skills we learn when we are younger are the skills that we learn in school such as writing, arithmetic, how to listen and things of that nature. Others are learned outside of school as we get older. They can come in the form of a hobby such as crocheting or sewing, or it can be something that's learned such as dancing or singing. When we recognize our strengths and skills, we can use them to find the passion we're seeking in our lives. Remember the example of languages. You could find that you have a talent for learning languages quickly. That would be a good strength or skill as it is also defined. While you would learn the languages and use that skill, you could find your passion being realized and discover the happiness of finding passion out of a good skill. So then, because it is making you happy, you want to keep doing it and you get better at it while you're learning.

Chapter Four: Identifying What You Love and Your Skill Set

One thing to recognize when you are looking at your life and attempting to realize what your passions are is that we need to realize the fact that sometimes, what we are good at, is not what we're passionate about. Many people assume that because they're good at something, they must be passionate about it. That's not always the case. Someone could be an amazing gymnast but hate it while they do it because of the long hours, harsh training schedule, or the toll it takes on their body.

Another good example would be someone who is an amazing singer but can't stand singing and wants to find something that they love doing and makes them happy rather than something they just happen to be good at. So, an important thing for us to distinguish is the difference between being passionate about something, and simply being good at something. Now, unfortunately, on the opposite side to that, what we're passionate about may not be something we're necessarily good at. Someone could want to be an opera singer but unfortunately, they may not have the skills necessary to achieve this dream. Or someone could want to be an actor, but they have horrible stage fright and are unable to speak in front of crowds. That doesn't mean they should give up on that dream though. It simply means that they need to work in this dream and use the skills they have to make it happen. It's very rare that someone is amazing at something the first time they try it. It's more likely and logical that we will have to work and not give up on what we're trying to achieve and remind ourselves to be patient so that we will be able to make it happen for ourselves.

In using critical thinking to help us find out what our passions are, I believe that an important first step is to think about the skills that you already have. A helpful tip is to realize and determine what skills you've learned from childhood, and which ones were learned from necessity. A perfect example of what a skill learned out of necessity looks like is that if you're a shy person and don't talk much but you're looking for a job. They tell you that if you're not able to communicate effectively, you won't get the job because you're going to have to talk to people. However, you're shy and that's incredibly difficult for you. In order to get hired for this job, you would most likely teach yourself effective communication skills, even though it would take a while because you're shy. Each individual person usually has many skills that they are good at. This helps us realize what we're best suited for but as I said before, just because you're good at it doesn't mean you're passionate about it. While some people learn to be passionate about it or find the passion later, some simply do not. It depends on each person and there is no right or wrong answer. A good thing to also consider is what made you happy as a child? Did you like reading? Climbing trees? Did you enjoy history or music? Oftentimes, the things we loved as children can translate into useful skills for the future.

The reason for this is that children were freer of the responsibilities that plague the adults. A good example here would be, Billy loves to learn about history as a child and it makes him happy when he's learning about past events. Because he loves to learn about it, he continues to read and learn thereby absorbing everything he can. As he goes through school or even college, his skill in learning is developing quickly because he loves what he's doing. In the future, this could turn into a job as a historian, an archeologist, or paleontologist, or a hundred other careers that deal with studying history and continuing with a subject he is passionate about. He'd be able to do this because he nurtured his gift and didn't quit. While continuing to learn new things and challenge himself in a professional career, he is following his passions and is happy in his choices.

Another example could be that Suzy loves playing the violin. She's not very good at it, but it really makes her happy and she loves the violin. She gets a little sad that she's not very good, but she is determined to get better at it and not give up on her dream. Over time, with careful studying and tutelage, she gets better and better and learns to perfect her craft. Because she didn't give up and continued to push for her dreams, she now has a career that she's not only passionate about but one that she's good at because she worked hard to achieve her dreams.

One of the things that are said to be a good reason for asking what made you happy as a child, is to think about it like this. Children don't have responsibilities, they are free to do whatever they wish, within reason of course. They still have to follow what their parents tell them to, but they don't have jobs or bills. They don't have to be up at six in the morning and come back late at night after a full day's work. They play and have fun and get to learn the things they really like to do. When my friend was young, she loved telling stories and had an amazing imagination. She read every book she could get her hands on and now she's a writer. Many people told her it wasn't a good idea, and that you don't make money with it which most people say is actually a reason that they don't pursue their passions. They are worried they can't be successful with it. What we should remember here is to never give up on our dreams and to keep pushing for the goals that we want.

Instead of letting other people influence you in a negative way, follow your heart. Don't let others tell you what you can and can't do with your life. If you're passionate about something, go for it. My friend didn't listen to the naysayers and instead, she followed her passions and is happy in the choices she made. When she was thinking about what she wanted to do in her life, she thought about what she liked when she was younger. She remembered when she was a teenager, she loved to write and to read, and those two things made her the happiest and it carried on into her adult life. When she began to write, it helped her to feel fulfilled in her life. She was excited to start right away and spends her days writing just like most people go to an office. The only difference is her job lets her wear pajamas if she doesn't feel like getting dressed professionally and she's happy to wake up every morning and go to work. She wakes up and instead of complaining about having to work, she is eager and excited to get started and sometimes doesn't stop until the day is completely gone.

This is why it's a good thing to think about for her skills and the things she loved as a child translated into a good career for her as an adult and it made her happy. Another trick is to think about what you would do if you didn't have anything holding you back? Now in life, we obviously have responsibilities, and nothing is perfect. But for the sake of the question, pretend for a moment that you don't have something holding you back. If you could do anything that you wanted, what would you do? This helps us realize things that were passionate about that you may not have thought about. You can use your thinking skills to work toward this passion if you'd like and turn it into a career for you, or if you think it would make a better hobby, that's fine too. Remember, there is no right or wrong answer here. It is about discovering skills that can help you in your daily life and help make your decisions easier. Critical thinking helps us make these decisions with logic and it helps us lessen the chance of negative impact because of our actions in whatever you decide to choose or do, whatever works for you, and the situation you are in.

Another good question is to ask yourself what your strengths are. Are you good at communicating with people? A good typist? A good musician? These skills can also help you determine which career might be right for you as well. Another thing to consider though is if you are good at typing but hate doing it, you're not going to be passionate about jobs where you would spend hours at a time typing. In fact, the opposite might happen, and you might hate your job, or dread going to work because you're doing something you can't stand. Another example would be, let's say you're an amazing salesperson. You can sell anything to anyone. So, you think because you're good at selling things, a retail job is good for you. Not if you don't like doing it. If you don't like doing something, it can drain the energy out of you, make you tired or depressed, it can even make you bitter, and cause problems in other aspects in your life as well. So, it wouldn't be beneficial in any way for you to do something you don't like because all it would be doing for you is causing problems.

This goes back to the 'if you're good at it you but might not be passionate about it' scenario. A better avenue is to determine strengths that coincide with what makes you happy. Oftentimes, it said that the things we loved as a child can bring us the most passion as adults as discussed above. Perhaps you loved to dance, and you have a power and strength for it. This would be the perfect example of using your skills for something you are passionate about and loved doing as oftentimes, our strengths as a person can lead us to where our passions lie. It can be something you already know you have a passion for or something completely unexpected. For example, have you ever had a skill that you knew you were good at but never used it to its fullest extent? Think of it like this. You are really good at cooking. You're an ace in the kitchen but you never really thought about doing it much. Maybe, one day you're in the kitchen and you start to think about how much you actually like it, and that cooking relaxes you and makes you happy. You may have just found an unexpected passion from a skill you already have. As time goes on, you'd have fun making new food and learning new things, or you could find a sense of accomplishment or pride when you make a meal which could, in turn, make your mood improve.

Is there an activity you love doing and hate to stop? Can you think of an activity that you do and then you lose yourself in it? Can you sit in a comfy chair and read for hours and not realize the time has passed? Or do you enjoy working on cars in the garage and not realize hours have gone away? Maybe you love bike riding into the sunset, and before you realize it, your time has gone. If you're unsure, take some time to really think about it. If it helps, make a list of all the things you hate doing, and then make a list of things you do like doing. Or even a list of things you've always wanted to try but never been able to do before. That is actually a good way to discover things you're passionate about but never got to experience. It's also a really good way to determine what you're doing in the daily life that you already like doing.

This might seem like an obvious thing to say. That you should think about things that you like to determine things that you're passionate about, but it will help in the future. Most people don't think about what they spend their time doing. When you begin to think about the activities you get lost in, you can realize the activities that you can spend most of your day doing. The reason this is helpful is that it's highly unlikely that you would spend a good portion of your day doing something you don't like. Therefore, it's easy to determine from thinking about this what you could be passionate about and enjoy doing to make your days better and more productive.

Using your steps to critical thinking, you should be able to narrow down choices right away. Remembering the step by step process and thinking of the evidence of your choices, it should be easy to eliminate choices from your list. If you can't, that's still alright. Remember, learning how to become a better critical thinker takes time. For some people, it doesn't happen right away as does figuring out what your passions are. But utilizing your thinking skills should, at the very least, narrow down your search to a considerable amount so that you're not becoming overwhelmed with your choices or figuring out what you really want and you're better able to concentrate.

This leads to another question. What do you really want? This may seem like an obvious question but it's not. This is actually a hard question for a lot of people and most answer with 'I don't know what I really want'. Which leads to the question that's usually tied to that question. How do you know that you don't know what you want? Take time and really think about this. Learning what you really want is one of the most important questions you can ask yourself and it's just as important to be honest with yourself. Determining what you really want is how you realize where your passions lie. It can be hard admitting what you want but it will help you in realizing your strengths as well as the passion you seek.

In some cases, we're completely blind to our own strengths and passions. They could be staring us right in the face, but we just can't see it. This once again goes back to thinking about things objectively and logically while thinking things point by point. Weigh the possible negative impacts and conflicts from our choices. You can even think about what people tell you. Do you get complimented for your baking skills? Do people fawn all over you when you sew a dress? Oftentimes, things that people compliment us on are also things that we could be passionate about but we're just not seeing it. As critical thinking can also help us become more self-aware, it is easier to see the routine activities that we could be missing simply because we're overlooking it.

On the other side to this coin, if people keep complimenting you on something you don't like doing and don't want to do, you shouldn't keep doing it simply because people want you to. You should make your own decisions and determine what you want to do for yourself. Baking, for example, is something that a lot of people can do, and their creations are delicious. A person might share with their friends and they are constantly praising her for her good food. Maybe she hates baking but only does it because her friends and family are so sweet with their praise. It's nice to do nice things for other people but don't make yourself miserable if you don't truly enjoy doing something. You should do the things you actually like to do instead of wasting time on things that you don't.

With all the advances in technology that's available, there are even quizzes online that can help you realize things about yourself that you may not have realized. Learning to put your critical thinking to use here, you can determine what would be false or true and what suits you and what doesn't. These quizzes are designed for a mass amount of people and while they have several answers, what you get on a quiz isn't always right. Sometimes you can take one and the answer you get is good and makes you think about things in a new light. Others don't. If you take a quiz on food and it tells you that your favorite food is chocolate ice cream, but you can't eat ice cream, that's a perfect example of the quiz not knowing you. If you take one about traits and it said that you're an innovative thinker and leader and that seems more like you, then it was probably a good quiz to take. A really interesting thing though is when you get a result that makes you think about things you'd never considered before. Like, am I more caring, or intelligent? Am I a philanthropist, or humanitarian?

What are you? Are you a nurturer? Inventor? A leader or a follower? Learning these things can all help point you to the right path of discovering where your passions lie and its good self-discovery. Take a look at your life and think objectively. Are you happiest when you help others? Are you happiest alone? Do you like mentoring people? Remember, in critical thinking, we need to identify the facts and logically conclude what it is we're learning. Question the information in front of you before blindly accepting. You have a point you are trying to discover or make and need to think it through systematically going through the facts you're presented with.

Remember, critical thinking isn't always easy because it forces you to take a hard look at yourself and force you to learn your weaknesses and strengths. The benefits are that you can learn who you are as a person and see where your passion lies. Learning one's weaknesses and strengths can help teach us where we belong and what we can do to make our lives more fulfilled. We can learn from our weaknesses and become stronger and likewise, there is much to learn from the strengths we already have. It could be that something you're weak in is actually something that can help you in the passion you wish to achieve.

Remember the example we used before? With Suzy and the violin? She had a passion for the music but was weak in skill or strength. So, she worked hard and persevered in her choices and then eventually became much better thereby lighting her passion even further and making herself happy. In the example of Billy, he was strong in his ability to learn but even with his chosen career, he was able to keep challenging himself and learn new things every day so that he wouldn't get bored. We learn from our weaknesses and our strengths both combined. There is always more we can learn about ourselves and things we can work on. It helps us improve ourselves daily and become better and better.

For some, they already know where their passion and skill sets lie. That's fine, but critical thinking can still play a part in helping you to actually utilize those passions and help you become happier. Which passion are you more excited about? Which one do you want to pursue actively? For some people, the idea of money holds them back. For example, someone could be passionate about becoming a writer and think that it's not financially responsible. But when you look at all the possibilities for writing today, you'll actually realize you can make a lot of money with it because there are literally hundreds of different routes to take. Likewise, say someone was passionate about handmaking jewelry but thinks this would be a horrible idea because it seems like it would be irresponsible. Research can help you find thousands of jobs for this as well. In some cases, we don't have many options that are true, however, in any case, research can show us that there are many more options than we realize, and we simply have to take the time to do the work and find them.

A good trick, if you're a visual person, to help determine where your strengths and passions lie is to make a list. Take two sheets of paper and on one write your skills and on another write your passions. You could even take a third sheet and begin to write all of the things you'd like to try. Most people find a hidden passion from trying something they'd never tried before. A college student, for example, might be so busy with their schedules and classes that they don't have that much time to devote to cooking or trying new recipes. Once they got a chance to try cooking though, they might find that they love it and quickly devote their time to it as their passion for it rises. Another person might not be able to swim, but on a whim decides to try. They might find that they love swimming and begin to do it every day because they find they like it so much. They may even turn into a 'mermaid' never leaving the water because they find swimming so enjoyable.

Others are held back because they have more than one passion. That is not something that should hold you back but excite you. There's no rule that says you're limited to one. Many people are passionate about a lot of things and it would be impossible and maybe even detrimental to eliminate all but one. People with many passions come alive from doing many different things and there is nothing wrong at all about that. In fact, having many passions can be just as beneficial as having one. It depends on the type of person you are. Some people prefer having one passion or thing to pursue wholeheartedly others enjoy a faster pace and like more hobbies or passions to fulfill their time.

One thing to remember is that there are as many different things to try as there are people on this planet and you can have a lot of fun trying them out and seeing what you like and what you don't, what you're good at, and what you're not. Like in the example of Suzy though, if you like doing something, just because you're not good at something right away it doesn't mean you have to give it up. Keep trying and you can get better. Remember applying your critical thinking here. It will help you determine your best skills and passions. While you're learning what you like and what you don't, think logically and systematically about the decisions and choices that you're making. It will help guide you on your search to reaching for your passions and will help you figure out what avenues to pursue no matter what choice you decide to make.

Chapter Five: Fun Tips for Finding and Discovering Your Passion and How Critical Thinking Helps the Process

To discover our passions, we've been talking about critical thinking and how to use these steps to find them, and then try to achieve them. Finding our passions can be a fun experience and even though critical thinking is a deep process, you can still have fun with it. There are a lot of interesting and unique ways to use critical thinking to help you find out what you love to do and where that love leads you.

20 Questions

Try playing twenty questions with yourself. If you need a good starter list, check the end of this book. The list of questions is designed to help you take a critical look at yourself while using the skills we've been talking about. By using the skills outlined, the list of questions can help you on your way to determining your strengths and passions and help you recognize some you probably already have. This is a really good list with reasons why each one is a good question for you to think about. Use the steps we've outlined to really consider your answers and weigh the pros and cons. Remember the logical thinking that makes us more self-aware in our thoughts and ideas. Using the steps that we've outlined can also remind you of lessening the negative impact or consequences of your decisions.

Passion Board

Make a passion board. The same concept as a creativity board but instead, use it for things you like to do. It will help you figure out what your passions are or what they could be. What interests you? What do you like to see and read about? What do you like to do? Put it on the board. Once you fill it up, you can see that you probably put things in there that you didn't even think you were actually passionate about. Like traveling. Some people think they are too busy or it's not something that interests them, then they look at their passion board and realize they have an entire space dedicated to pictures of tropical beaches or mountains and other places they'd like to visit. This is the reason a passion board is a good idea. It helps us realize things we didn't know about ourselves. If you're not realizing a new passion, maybe, you're realizing an old passion that you forgot you had. Now that you've realized it again, you can pick it back up and see if you're still interested in that passion or if it's something you've moved on from. On the same point, the passions you didn't realize that you had or that you were interested in, you can take those up as well and begin to follow those passions as well. This is a really good idea to combine old and new and it's a fun way to see the things you really want to pursue.

Make a People List

The people list is a good way for you to think about inspiration. Think of the people that inspire you and make a list of who they are. Are they where you want to be? Have they done something with their lives that you wish you could have or want to? If you know your passion, that's great! If not, that's okay too. Either way, the people on your list can make you think and that's exactly what we want to achieve. These people are successful and there is something about them that you admire and respect. Maybe it's something they've done in their career or something in their regular life.

You can use this list to help you realize how they inspire you. It can also help you realize what you like to do in life and how you can make it happen for yourself. If your inspiration is a famous actor, for instance, think about what it is about them you like. Do you like the fact that they are able to follow their passion? Or do they help a lot of people in their spare time? Think logically about your list and really think about why these people are on it. This is going to help you realize where your passions lie and seeing other people in the field or passion that you want for yourself, you can have continued inspiration for how to achieve it for yourself. You could even use these people as role models if you choose to.

20 Activities List

Like twenty questions, this list is super fun and helps you realize what you like to do, day or night. List twenty activities that you enjoy doing on a daily basis and then list how often you do it and the positives and negatives of your list. For example, the first thing on your list could be that you enjoy television. Now, to coincide with what we just said, write how often you do it daily and how much pleasure you get from said activity. Is it free or expensive? Television is actually cheap depending on how you do it, but it still costs money. Now that's alright. If you're willing to spend money on things you love to do, that's completely fine.

If some of the activities you do costs too much, you can reevaluate it and see if it needs to be redone. The reason I say this is that different people have different circumstances and for some people, they would rather take out a luxury than sacrifice a passion. You'll find that when you list your activities and see what it is your spending your days doing, that you'll be able to see what you like and what you don't. Realizing what you like and what you don't can help you better come to the realization of what you're passionate about and what you're not. Then you can start to realize which passions you want to pursue in the future and which activities you're willing to let go. Or you can start seeing activities that you wish you could do more often but don't or new activities you're willing to try for yourself.

List of Like

This is a list of why you like yourself. Or, more specifically, you're going to pick fourteen words that describe why you like yourself. Are you playful? Kind? Sweet? Take your time and list fourteen things about yourself that you like. Once you have that list written down, you can use critical thinking to see what you're good at. This goes back to the 'strength can lead to passion' chapter because, in the exercises listed above, it's about finding your passion. This exercise, I believe, would do both. This exercise will help you see the things you like about yourself and usually, the things we like about ourselves can be linked to strengths that we have. Maybe we don't realize the strengths inside us, but they are there and exercises like these can help show you what they are. We all have inner strength and sometimes we just don't know what they are. Activities like this can bring them to the light and help us learn more about ourselves.

Then you can go from there. You have a list of things you're good at and by thinking critically on those things, you can find things from there that you're passionate about and want to achieve or things that you'd like to learn more about. You can then begin trying the activities or ideas from your list and start to see what makes you happiest and the most fulfilled in your life.

No Failing

What would you do if you knew that there was zero chance of you failing? Most people hesitate to find their passions or pursue them because they have so many obstacles in their path. Money is an issue or time is an issue. Or there is the threat of failure or a hundred other reasons that can stop you from achieving or even recognizing what it is you're trying to discover or set out to do. Sometimes we can just be afraid. But what if you could eliminate all that? That's the purpose of this activity. If you had no obstacles whatsoever and no chance of failing, what do you think you would do in your life?

Is it something you never would have thought of? Or something you have but didn't think it was possible? Being able to think about this without the threat of the obstacles looming over your head, it becomes easier to see what it is you are passionate about. Maybe you answered I don't know when you saw this question. Look deeper. Think for a long moment about what you really want to do. This activity isn't made to upset or irritate anyone, it simply meant to make you envision what you're passionate about with nothing holding you back. It can show you options that you never considered in the past or bring back something that you did. Maybe you thought of something really special that you've always wanted to do and never told yourself you really wanted it. Or just something that's always been on your mind and this just confirms it. Whatever scenario you find yourself in, you will be able to see what your passion is and utilizing your critical thinking skills can help make your passion a reality.

Think Back

The think back exercise is where you think back to your childhood and remember what you liked to do then. It's been mentioned earlier because this really can help you discover passions that you had and don't anymore or that you had and still have. Like the 'no failing exercise', the 'think back' basically eliminates most of the obstacles surrounding what you want to do simply because when you're a child, you don't have any obstacles. When you're a child, you can laugh and have fun. Your meals are provided for you, you have a place to live, you don't have to worry about anything because your parents provide it all for you.

As an adult, we can be weighed down by everything in our lives and sometimes we need to take a step back and think for a moment. Sometimes taking that moment to stop and think can really help us. This is what critical thinking is all about. Here, critical thinking can really come into play because you're stepping back and thinking things through and evaluating your choices and thoughts. Another reason this is such a good activity to do and think about is that it takes you back to a time when you imagined yourself as anything you wanted to be and didn't have to think about if it was possible or not. You simply believed you could do anything or be anything. Thinking about things like that helps us realize our passions and strengths now as well as then.

A good example here would be the writer once again. My friend was searching for her passion and purpose in her life and sat down for a long time, unspeaking, just thinking. She thought about what made her happy as a child and remembered she was always writing stories and songs. She realized that when she was younger, this was the thing that made her happiest. So, she began writing as an adult. She didn't listen to anyone else or any negative influences. She simply followed her heart and her passion, and it led her back to writing. At first, she wasn't sure what writer she wanted to be and started out with different avenues to see what she liked best.

She discovered that she didn't like writing long books unless they were her own because she would start to feel drained, but she enjoyed writing small things like blog posts or articles. Through trial and error, she was quickly able to see what it was she really liked to write about. Eventually, the negative influences faded away, but it didn't matter if they did or not as she wasn't listening anymore. When she let go of the negative influences, she was able to let her passion reign free and write to her heart's content. She'd found her passion and was pursuing it steadily and happily. This is a great example of not only going back to your childhood to see what you love and where your passions truly lie, but it's also a good example of removing the negatives in your life because they don't help you. The negative influences in your life bring you down and make you doubt what you really want even if you already know it.

Do Things You Like

If you haven't figured out your passion yet, that's ok. Remember, this is a process, not a two-minute thing or something that can happen right away. Self-discovery takes time and patience. This activity might help though. Remember the list of like? This can tie into that. We already have a list of the things we like to do. Now, utilize your thinking skills and do the things you like to do. Do the things that bring you enjoyment and happiness. When you figure out what you like and start doing it, you can quickly understand how the things you already like to do can lead to passion. If you're someone who enjoys crocheting as a hobby, you could sit down and do that but then, maybe, as you do it more and more, you realize, "Hey, this isn't just a hobby anymore. This is something I really care about doing! This is something that makes me really happy and I enjoy being able to do it." When we spend our time doing things we like, we learn better ways of making ourselves happy which is a positive benefit to finding out what passions you have or are developing.

Another benefit of finding your passions and doing things that you like to do is that it can make you a happier person. When you're spending time doing things you like instead of wasting time doing things you don't, you can find that you're much less stressed because you're doing things for yourself. You're taking time for you. Everyone needs a little time for them and that's alright. Do the things you like to do, and you will find that your mood is improving, and you might feel like you have more purpose or that your time is used more wisely.

Themes in Life

This activity deals with themes. Think of your life. All of it. From your career, your hobbies, everything. Even dating or things like that. Do you notice any themes going on? If there is a reoccurring theme or themes, this can point to habits or things you already had in place or were already interested in. Do you read a lot of travel magazines? Watch a lot of judge shows on tv? Maybe your passion lies in travel and you want to see and explore new places with family and friends or take a really cool vacation by yourself. Maybe sandy beaches or a tropical island is what you've been craving.

Or maybe, the law is what attracts your attention. Do you like the judge shows because they're funny or do you find yourself thinking about how the situation should be handled and it's not? Or how you could do it better? Do you buy the same types of things over and over? Like makeup or bath products? Now for this one, the latter can be looked at two ways. We can always use bath products because we need to bathe every day. For this example, I am talking about extra items that you don't necessarily need. Do you constantly buy bath bombs or things of that nature? Organic soaps or shampoos or what about body oils? You might be surprised but just paying attention to your purchases can lead you to see something that you might like to do or have a passion for. A love of makeup could lead to internet videos or cosmetology or a whole branch of different ideas. A love of fragrant soaps or body oils could turn into a beauty shop or at home business. There are so many unique and fun ways to learn about how to find our passion and though some like this one might seem odd, it could actually help. Sometimes, it's the things you think wouldn't be very helpful but then you try it and it is.

Some people spent outrageous amounts of money on video games and gaming systems. They love playing games and spend hours lost in the shooting, or different worlds, or capturing a medical horned monster kidnapping the princess. What they don't realize is that this could be a major passion that could lead to some pretty cool opportunities for your future. Did you know that people can get paid to play games all day? Or they could get sponsored by a company and get paid to play their games exclusively. You can use the critical thinking skills here too. Think hard about the best decision for you that will yield the most positive results. What is going to make you the happiest and be the most beneficial in your life?

Journal

In the previous chapters, I had mentioned journaling your experiences so you could see how to correct them with critical thinking. Everyone had a moment where they've argued with someone and said, 'why didn't I say this or that' and you get upset. We discussed that journaling the situation can help you over time. It'll be able to fix that thought process because over time, you would start to get better with utilizing your critical thinking process and start to see how you want the conversation to go while you're having it instead of rehashing it later.

Now, I'm suggesting journaling for other reasons as well. I had mentioned before that a journal can be more than just a place to write your feelings or innermost secrets, and it is, but it can also be used for exactly just that and it can be massively beneficial. When we don't have a set agenda, we tend to write much more freely. We don't have negative influences crowding our minds such as social media or fake friends, no peer pressure, just you and the page. You can speak your innermost thoughts here and discover what you want out of your life and your thinking skills once again help you stay systematic and logical. Spending time writing your thoughts or feelings and being able to express yourself freely is so important to help us find who we are and our passions in life.

Remember, the media and everything around us have so much information every single second of every day. It can be very hard to understand the truth and what's not because there is simply too much of it around us. It would be impossible to see and hear it all. We also have the influence of our family, our friends, and coworkers. Everyone around you can affect you. Am I saying they're all bad influences? Of course not. In fact, many of them are probably very good influences that you should have around you. What I am saying is imagine how it would feel to simply unplug and write without their influence but yourself. You will see things more clearly and probably be amazed at how you feel when no one is influencing you and you're able to write whatever you wish and let everything you need to let out on the page.

Superhero!

One of my favorite activities is the superhero. This activity can be so much fun for people to do and I think we can all agree. We could all use a little more fun. Close your eyes and imagine yourself about to go to work. Not so fast. You're probably imagining the job you go to every day and that's not what we're wanting here. You're going on your dream job today. If you are already working the job of your dreams, that's awesome! You can imagine the job you work every day then. But for those who haven't found their perfect job yet, this can work really well for you. Close your eyes and imagine your dream job. Now go ahead. Visualize it. You're getting ready to go to work and it's the job you've always wanted. So, where are you going to work today? Are you a superhero? Most people probably won't really imagine this since people in capes flying around planets and saving people on a daily basis don't actually exist. But maybe, you're imagining a different type of superhero. A real one that we do see in the day to day life.

Are you imagining yourself as a firefighter saving a burning building, or maybe a doctor finishing a lifesaving surgery and bringing joy to a family? You could be imagining becoming a teacher and educating the minds of young people giving them new opportunities and enriching an entire new generation's mind. Not all superheroes wear capes. This exercise will help you discover your superhero and help you think of what you really want to be. Whatever it is your imagining, it could be a secret passion or more likely a skill you haven't yet learned. It's a fun and useful tool to help us think about passions we might have set aside and not realized. Now that you can be anything you want to be, let your imagination take you away for a moment and picture who you really want to be. Then you can decide to follow your passion and begin to make it happen.

Go!

Like the title implies, go is go. If you've already discovered your passion, this one is especially true for you. Instead of talking about what you're going to do or thinking about what you're going to do, get up and do it. Take some action for your passion. Many people will discover that they have a little bit of the 'doer' inside them. A doer is just like it sounds. They do things. Remember when you were in school and they talk about the different ways people learn?

Seeing, hearing, or doing? That's just what doers are able to do. They operate best by getting up and doing the things they want to learn or do. They don't wait around. For our passion, this could be anything from taking a class to reading an article or blog post. It doesn't have to be a big thing right away. It can be if that's what you would like to do. It can be big or small. For most people, change can be really hard and doing too much too quickly is overwhelming, to say the least. If that sounds like you, you can start small with a blog post or something easy like that. No muss no fuss. You're behind a computer screen in your own home. Not much can freak you out, right? This is a good thing. Some people have anxiety with things like this and starting small is much better for them.

For others who are ready for a big step, maybe they would like to take a class and meet new people interested in the same activities they are. Either option is fine. Like we said before, there is no right or wrong answer when it comes to finding your passion, critical thinking, and self-discovery. Some people are introverts, while others are extroverts. Obviously, since everyone is different, they would have to approach this in different ways, whatever works the best for you as an individual. The purpose of these exercises is to use your critical thinking to become more self-aware and to help you find your passions. Whether you are ready for big steps or tiny steps, it's alright. You may decide that maybe, both suit you and go back and forth between the two until you're comfortable. This is an interesting approach as well. Whatever way we decide to go about it, the important thing is, for the sake of this exercise, is to get up and go.

Let's Get Involved

For this activity, we should submerge ourselves. If you already found your passion or at least know of one passion that you have, get involved. Take a class or a workshop that's related to your passion. If you love pottery go, take a pottery class. Meet up with people that have the same interests as you do and have fun doing it. How about volunteering in what you're interested in? Or even talk to people who have made a career from doing this? It can help broaden your horizons and really teach you something new about what you really care about in ways you didn't know about.

A lot of times, speaking with someone who has years of experience doing something can be a really good teacher and help us realize things about our passions that we might not have been able to figure out on our own. It's probable that we would have but it's still nice to have someone experienced to talk to that can help you with any questions you have or stories that can spark your passion further. Networking and seminars are also a great place to learn about passions and these days, our society has them for everything as we live in the digital age. Find one for your passion and be ready to learn new things that you can try later. Or, maybe, attending a seminar can get you a really good career opportunity with something you really care about doing. This activity is designed to help you discover ways to follow your passion and make you happy while letting you work toward something you care about instead of something that you don't. Remember what we said earlier. If you don't like doing something, there's no point in doing it. Use your time wisely and fill it up with the things you do care about doing. Getting involved can open so many doors that may not have been accessible to you before, but you'll notice when you try, maybe two or three open all at once.

Vision Board

Like the passion board, this is going to help you figure out what you want, but this goes one step further. In the passion board, you were figuring out what your passions were. In the vision board, we're working on passions you already have and we're trying to make them happen. So, fill your board with ideas about how you're going to take the passions you have and make them a reality. For example, you love traveling and want to go to another country. That's a good passion and many people love to travel. How are you going to make it happen? Put it on the board. You can go step by step, brainstorming or any combination of techniques you like. Just remember to utilize your critical thinking skills while you do this. You'll be able to see a pathway that leads you to your passion and shows you how it can be obtained. This is especially helpful because one of the things we're trying to do here is to discover our passions and then achieve them so that we can be happier in our lives.

The steps of critical thinking are so that we can think logically about what we're doing and begin to achieve the things that we wish. This is why the vision board is so helpful. We can see the steps one by one that we're trying to complete to be able to follow our passions once we have found them. After we've achieved them, we have a sense of accomplishment that we were able to do what we set out to do and we could make this happen for ourselves thanks to our critical thinking.

Never Quit

This one is pretty easy to understand. Never quit trying. Success is not an overnight thing and like we've said many times, this critical thinking isn't easy. But it's worth the effort you put into it as well. How much more will you appreciate your success when you know you pushed yourself as hard as you could and didn't give up? Don't let others influence you negatively. Think calmly and objectively using the skills that you've learned in this book once again. You'll find your passions and success by not giving up or quitting for any reason. When you reach that goal line, you'll know that it was your strength and determination that led you there and the prize will be that much sweeter because you were the one that got yourself there.

Chapter Six: 20 Questions to Help You Determine Your Passions and Strengths

1) What Did You Enjoy Doing as a Child?

This is a useful question because, in many cases, the things we enjoyed when we were carefree, innocent, without the pressure of responsibility or money, things that adults face and children don't, are also the things that we are interested in now as adults. Or maybe, you loved something as a child and don't do it anymore as an adult but wish you could and feel like you're not able to.

2) How Have You Faced Challenges in Your Life?

Everyone in their life has faced challenges at some point or another and realizing how you dealt with it helps you realize what strengths you used to overcome the challenges you were facing. Do you still solve problems the same way? Has anything changed? When you're faced with a problem, how do you get through it? This question really makes you think about how you used your strengths to face the problems you have in your life. Thinking about these things also helps you realize your strengths from before in your life to the strengths you have now and if you're able to face challenges better because of them.

3) Do You Have Any Unusual Skills?

This question helps you think about how you're different from other people. Take a few moments and really think about this. It will help you realize some underlying strengths that you process that you may not have realized you have. Some people can type with their feet, others can do the splits, and some people can do acrobatics. Everyone has something about them that makes them different and this is a good way to determine interesting skills that you have. These strengths will show you that you're unique and an individual. You can find that when you're thinking about this, you could have many skills you didn't realize you could do.

4) What Do You Yearn to Do?

Thinking about you are yearning to do makes you realize things that you're not doing but really want to thereby help you realize your passions, and it can also help you realize undeveloped talents or even unexplored and undiscovered talents. When thinking about this, you can find a talent that you haven't really been able to peruse but want to, or something that you've never tried, but are really good at.

5) If All of the Problems in Your life Were Solved, What Do You Think You Would Do?

There are many things that people would do if we were free enough to make the choice. Now, obviously, this is hypothetical as many people have issues and responsibilities in their life that cannot be ignored such as money and bills or things of that nature, so all of our problems will most likely not be fixed when your reading this question. But for the sake of the question, pretend you have no problems at all. If free enough to make the choice, what would you do?

6) What Makes You Come Alive?

In your life, when you think about what makes you come alive, you can begin to realize what ignites your passion and makes your soul come alive. You'll begin to see the things you love and truly enjoy in your life and find the passions that ignite your heart. It may take some deep thinking to realize what these things are but seeing the things you really want and the things that truly make you happy will be a huge benefit to finding and following your passion.

7) What Do You Enjoy Doing?

This ties back into question number 6, however, where question 6 and 7 would help you find your passions and strengths, I believe question 6 would help more with finding your passions, while I believe question 7 would help more with finding your strengths. If it helps, make a list of what you enjoy doing so you can have something to see and think about. This helps especially if you're a visual person because it is laid out in front of you and helps you picture it better. And, in the case of a lot of people, writing things down helps. It makes it more solid and real, and you can have it to go back to whenever you need it. Similar to the journal idea that is mentioned in the previous chapters, this method of being able to see it should help with making you realize what you enjoy doing.

8) What Was Your First Achievement?

As an adult, this might seem like it's not very important at all because your childhood was years and years ago, but it really is a good question to think about. No matter how small or even boring this achievement might seem to you, thinking about your early achievement and how you set about achieving it is going to give you pointers to your innermost strengths. While there are strengths that are obvious to us and some that aren't, our innermost strengths can be an amazing eye-opener to us and help us realize things we hadn't before.

9) What Brings You the Most Satisfaction in Your Life?

This question will also help you determine what in your life brings you happiness and joy. The things that bring you satisfaction in your life can help you figure out what you're passionate about because it will be the things that help you realize when you're pleased and happy with others and yourself.

10) When You Lose Track of Time, What Is Something That You Find Yourself Immersed In?

This will help you realize what you enjoy doing so much that you lose yourself in it. You can see what you have a real passion for, and what really makes you happy to do. For some people, they read for hours and don't even realize how much time has gone by, or others love to knit and have an entire project done before they look up and notice the time. What do you immerse yourself in?

11) Can You Think of a Worldly Problem That You Would like to Fix?

By identifying what you care about in the world, it can also reveal new things about yourself you didn't know. The process of critical thinking helps us become more aware and insightful and this question utilizes that by having you think about the world. You could discover that maybe, you're passionate about humanitarianism or animal rights, philanthropy, or helping children. There're many ways this question can help you discover your passions, but it can also help you discover strengths and you could help other people while making yourself happy as well.

12) What Do You Get Complimented on the Most?

This question will help you think about what others like about you and what they admire about you. This can help you look for untapped strengths and skills that others see in you and can help you recognize them in yourself as well as maybe finding a passion you hadn't realized before in yourself. Often times, people don't realize that they are really good at something until someone else makes them aware of it. If that's the case for you, think about what people compliment you on.

13) What Are Things You Do for Friends or Family, Workers or Other People in Your Life, That They Seek Your Input For?

You might realize that things you already do for people in your life involve a lot of strengths you didn't realize you have. Helping people takes a lot and most people don't realize how much strength it takes to help people sometimes. It can take a lot of you or it can make you realize things about yourself you hadn't thought of. This question makes you think about what strengths you utilize to help the people you love and care about and you might find that helping people could turn into a passion which gives you a lot of options for careers or other options you can enjoy.

14) What Do You Like About Yourself?

This one may be hard. Remember that the process of critical thinking has us look at ourselves and recognize not just our strengths but our weaknesses as well and for a lot of people, that is not an easy task. This question lets us think about ourselves. The reason this is a good question for people is that at just the basic level, the things we like about ourselves are usually a lot of the things we're good at which gives us a lot of options for understanding passion. At a deeper level, it can help with your self-esteem, help you realize possible passions, and help you realize what an awesome person you are.

15) Is There Someone Who Inspires You by

What They Do or the Way They Live Their Life?

Think about the people that you've studied in your life and that you admire. Even in school, for years you had to learn about famous people and how they lived. From presidents to abolitionists, to famous warriors and kings. Find one you admire. Or a lot of people you admire. Then think for a moment. They have qualities about themselves that you like and that interests you. Think about what those qualities are about them that you like. Is there something they do that you'd like to do? Something that they're interested in that maybe you are too? Or maybe they have a set of strengths that you admire as well. In another case, it could be that they've done something really meaningful in their life that you really look up to them for. Something that you would like to do in your own life. Using the step by step process of critical thinking, you can see which strengths and passions you have that they have or what they have that you'd like to have.

16) Do You Have a Bucket List?

This is a really fun way to learn about your passions and what sets your soul alive. You can write as many or as few as you want. Some people have as many as four hundred items on their list, some have as few as ten. It all depends on your own personal desires. There is no right or wrong here. It depends on your own personal wants. There is no wrong way to write this list and there is no wrong in writing however many you choose. But the really nice thing is that in writing this list, you'll get to see what you really want to do, and it will help you realize your passions and new strengths or old strengths. A really cool thing about this option as well is that certain things that you put on this list may let other people do them with you creating lasting memories that you'll be able to enjoy for the rest of your life.

17) What Do You Love or Enjoy Learning the

Most and Study About?

This one may seem obvious but surprisingly, not a lot of people think about this one. I think it really deserves some good thought. What do you like learning about? When you have to study, what do you enjoy and what do you dislike? Is there a certain subject that really excites and motivates you? Something that you could sit and learn about for hours? Something that we really love to study could lead the way in finding what we love and enjoy doing.

18) What Is Something That You'd like to Be Remembered or Known For?

This question really gets you to think because you must think about your future. Everyone has a way they want people to remember them and obviously, we want to be remembered for the best of us. Our good qualities are what we wish people to see and remember. Now, everyone makes mistakes, and no one is perfect, but think about how you'd like to be remembered. This could actually jumpstart your brain and heart into discovering a new passion and strength inside you. You could discover a whole new side of you that you'd never known about before.

19) Is There Something in Your Life That You Could Talk About for Hours?

This would be a really good question to determine if you already have something in your life that you're passionate about. When you think about what you could talk to your friends or family for hours nonstop, that's a really good indicator since it's something you really care about and it's something that you're really passionate about. Think back to high school when you were with your friends and you talked during breaks and lunch and there was never enough time to talk because you had so much you wanted to say. Just like adults now. If there is something that we really care about, we are able to freely communicate and be happy about it while wanting to share it with other people. We get so excited telling them and while we share about something for a good period of time, it shows us that this is something that would make us happy and therefore could be a really good passion of ours.

20) Are There Any Causes You like or Feel Drawn To?

This kind of ties into question 11 and a little of 19, but question 19 is for anything that you could feel passionate about. This one is asking for a cause you feel drawn to hence it is tied into 11 because question 11 asks what world problem you would like to fix. Today, we have thousands of causes that people could be passionate about. Anything from aids to hunger, homelessness, missing children, military, and all sorts of causes. This world needs help and it needs passionate people to help out. Is there one that speaks to you? Maybe you feel that women are being treated unfairly or that animals shouldn't live in cages. Whatever it is, because you feel drawn to it, it can spark passion, show you what moves you, and touches your soul. You can become a very passionate and involved person once you know where it is that your passions lie and what you love.

Don't miss out!

Visit the website below and you can sign up to receive emails whenever Steven West publishes a new book. There's no charge and no obligation.

https://books2read.com/r/B-A-EZVF-SFGAB

BOOKS 2 READ

Connecting independent readers to independent writers.

Did you love *Critical Thinking and Self-Awareness: How to Use Critical Thinking Skills to Find Your Passion: Plus 20 Questions You Must Ask Yourself?* Then you should read *Conscientiousness: How to Develop Conscientiousness, the Underlying Trait of Achievement and Business Success* by Steven West!

Are you Low in Conscientiousness?

Are you trying to achieve certain goals or build a business but find that you are not disciplined, are unorganized and procrastinate on the most important tasks? If you answered "YES!" then don't worry you are not alone, thousands of people struggle with these problems on a daily basis. The key to overcoming these problems is to increase your level of conscientiousness. You're about to discover the Underlying Trait of Achievement and Business Success

When You Download This Book Today You'll Also Learn...

What is ConscientiousnessImportance of Conscientiousness for Success and HappinessHow to be more organized even if you have never been beforeThe key to stop procrastinating and getting things done3 steps to increase self beliefMuch, much more!

Download your copy today!

Also by Steven West

Learn Memory Techniques - How to Learn Faster and Think More Clearly

Social Anxiety Detox Practical Solutions for Dealing with Everyday Anxiety, Fear, Awkwardness, Shyness and How to be Yourself in Social Situations

Conscientiousness: How to Develop Conscientiousness, the Underlying Trait of Achievement and Business Success

Assertiveness: Set Boundaries, Stand Up for Yourself, and Finally Get What You Want

Critical Thinking and Self-Awareness: How to Use Critical Thinking Skills to Find Your Passion: Plus 20 Questions You Must Ask Yourself

Made in the USA
Monee, IL
15 October 2020